SWEATY SUITS OF ARMOR

Could You Survive Being a Knight?

Chana Stiefel
Illustrated by Gerald Kelley

Enslow Publishers, Inc.
40 Industrial Road
Box 398
Berkeley Heights, NJ 07922
USA

http://www.enslow.com

Library of Congress Cataloging-in-Publication Data

Stiefel, Chana, 1968–
    Sweaty suits of armor : could you survive being a knight? / by Chana Stiefel.
       p. cm. — (Ye yucky Middle Ages)
    Includes bibliographical references and index.
    ISBN 978-0-7660-3784-7
    1. Knights and knighthood—Europe—History—Juvenile literature.
  2. Civilization, Medieval—Juvenile literature. I. Title.
    CR4513.S75 2011
    940.1—dc22
                    2010020758

Paperback ISBN 978-1-59845-376-8

Printed in the United States of America

042012 Lake Book Manufacturing, Inc., Melrose Park, IL

10 9 8 7 6 5 4 3 2

To Our Readers: We have done our best to make sure all Internet Addresses in this book were active and appropriate when we went to press. However, the author and the publisher have no control over and assume no liability for the material available on those Internet sites or on other Web sites they may link to. Any comments or suggestions can be sent by e-mail to comments@enslow.com or to the address on the back cover.

♻ Enslow Publishers, Inc., is committed to printing our books on recycled paper. The paper in every book contains 10% to 30% post-consumer waste (PCW). The cover board on the outside of each book contains 100% PCW. Our goal is to do our part to help young people and the environment too!

Illustration Credits: © 2010 Gerald Kelley, www.geraldkelley.com

Cover Illustration: © 2010 Gerald Kelley, www.geraldkelley.com

Contents

Could You Be a Knight?

Splat! You hit the mud face down. Good thing you are wearing a helmet. You've been knocked off your horse by a fierce-looking **knight**. The crowd goes wild. You're the new knight in town. You have to prove your bravery. All you need to do is shatter your wooden spear against the other knight's shield. In your heavy metal armor, you are baking under the blazing hot sun. At least under all that metal no one can see you sweat. If you win this contest, you could gain great fame and fortune. If you lose, well . . . You've practiced for this moment almost your entire life. No guts, no glory. You just hope you won't see any guts today—especially your own! Still, this contest beats fighting a nasty war that could go on for months.

Is this what you thought knighthood would be like? Charge back in time to find out what real life was like for knights of the Middle Ages.

Flashback

Knighthood was often sweaty, dirty, and bloody. When knights rode off to battle, they were headed for hand-to-hand combat against other powerful soldiers. They were trained to slash each other with swords. They pierced through metal armor with sharp spears. They hacked each other with axes. Some of them suffered deadly wounds. Infection, disease, and starvation were common on the battlefront. Sometimes the weather was freezing cold, and sometimes it was burning hot. Yet, if they survived, knights could be on a road to fame and fortune. Was it worth the risk?

The "glory days" of knighthood took place in Europe during the Middle Ages. This was a time from about the year 500 to the year 1500. These were often violent times. Armies fought each other over land. Knights were well trained warriors. Sometimes a knight was granted land by a wealthy lord. In return, the knight promised to fight in the lord's army. Knights would help guard a lord's castle. Some knights lived in their own castles. They ate at fancy feasts. Yet many knights were poor. A lord would give them horses and armor. They were paid to fight battles. They tried to win riches in war.

Get Ready!

The best way for knights to prepare for war was to fight in **tournaments**. These were mock battles. Spectators would flock to watch these "extreme sports." The tournaments could last for days. They could be just as dangerous and deadly as real combat.

Winners of tournaments received great riches. These included horses, weapons, and money from the knights who had lost. A winning knight could also hold his opponent for ransom (reward money). Some prizes were bizarre. Knights won wild bears, pigs, and even dead fish! Sometimes, as a reward, a knight would receive a kiss from one of the ladies of the court.

Melees were all the rage. These mock battles were extremely violent. In a melee, two teams of knights on horseback clashed against each other in an arena. The scene was total chaos: **lances** (sharp spears) jabbing, clubs swinging, horses colliding. The goal was to knock all the opposing knights off their horses. The winner was the last knight still mounted. In a melee, it was each man for himself. But sometimes knights would gang up on each other.

That's Using Your Head

One English knight, William Marshal (1147–1219), became famous for winning tournaments. After one particular victory, his squires found him at the blacksmith's shop. He was on his knees with his head resting on an anvil (a sturdy piece of iron). William had received so many blows to the head during the tournament that his helmet was twisted on backward. He needed a smith to help remove it!

In a **joust**, two mounted knights dueled against each other with lances. They tried to knock each other off their saddles. They also received points for shattering their lance against their opponent's shield. When their lances were broken, knights battled each other with swords, axes, or **maces**.

In one huge tournament in 1241 in Cologne, Germany, more than sixty knights were killed. Tournaments became so bloody that the Catholic Church banned them. Kings also tried to stop tournaments. Having so many powerful knights in one place was viewed as a threat. Yet many knights continued to compete. Certain safety measures were put in place. For example, sharp lances were replaced with blunt ones. A wooden barrier, called a **tilt**, was placed between jousting opponents so that their horses wouldn't collide.

Later on, tournaments were used more for entertainment than for practice. They were held at weddings or at political events. Still, the danger continued. In 1252, a knight named Arnold de Montigny was killed in a joust by another knight, Roger de Lemburn. Lemburn's lance was removed from Montigny's throat. The lance had not been blunted as it should have been. Lemburn was suspected of murder.

War at Its Worst

For several months each year, a knight had a duty to go to war for his lord. Some wars dragged on for years. Though they were tough and brave, knights had to put up with some nasty conditions. They often slept in tents on hard, rocky ground. In battle they had little protection from the boiling heat, bitter cold, or pouring rain.

Armies had no safe way to dispose of their poop. Diseases such as dysentery (severe diarrhea) spread through their camps. Just like the rest of the population, knights were exposed to **epidemics**. In the Middle Ages, widespread diseases included smallpox, cholera, and typhoid. In the mid-1300s an epidemic known as the **Black Death** wiped out 30 to 60 percent of the population of Europe. The Black Death was an infection carried by fleas living on rats. No amount of armor could protect knights from that dreaded disease.

Risky Business

Feeding a medieval army was a major challenge. Unlike today's soldiers, knights didn't receive MREs (Meals Ready to Eat). Medieval armies did bring food with them, but sometimes it ran out. Knights ate stale or moldy bread. They stole food from peasants. They drank from ponds and rivers. The water was often polluted by sewage. Like everyone else at the time, knights also chugged wine and beer.

The main risks, of course, were being wounded or killed by the enemy. Metal armor was good protection, but it was far from perfect. Imagine a knight is shot by an arrow. A doctor might try to pull it out. Yet there was no medicine to dull the pain. There was no drug to fight infection, either. Sometimes a doctor would "treat" a wound by burning it with a searing-hot iron!

13

If you were a wealthy knight, there was another danger: being captured. Capturing a wealthy knight and holding him for ransom was a big source of income in the Middle Ages. Sometimes, a knight's family would pay a year's salary—or more—for his release! The captured knight could be stripped of his expensive armor, weapons, horses, and all other precious belongings. But sometimes captive knights were treated like guests. If they swore not to escape, they were invited to banquets and on hunting trips. Other times, they were dragged

to the dark dungeons of castles. They were chained to the wall while waiting to be ransomed.

Surviving a Siege

A huge source of riches for knights was taking over castles. An army of mounted knights and foot soldiers might try to break down castle walls, climb over them, or tunnel beneath them. If the lord of the castle refused to surrender, the attacking army would lay siege, or surround the fortress. No food or supplies were allowed in or out. The strategy was to wear down the castle's residents through starvation. This could take months. During that time, knights and other soldiers could die of

In 1204, the French tried to capture Chateau Gaillard from the English. Some soldiers (probably troops with no sense of smell) climbed inside the castle through the stinky drains of the toilet!

hunger. So, they would take all the crops from the land outside the castle to feed themselves.

Sometimes the attackers would go to extremes. Armies used many kinds of catapults to fling huge boulders and balls of fire over castle walls. They even hurled over piles of poop, as

well as the rotting remains of dead animals! By doing so, they hoped to spread disease in the castle.

These tactics could spiral out of control. In 1159 the army of Frederick Barbarossa, the King of Germany, laid siege on the Italian city of Crema. Once, when Barbarossa left his camp for the day, six hundred knights from Crema led a surprise attack on the German troops. The battle was so deadly on both sides that the ground ran with blood. Barbarossa returned in a fury. His men chopped off the heads of dead knights. Then they played ball with them. In a rage, the city's defenders dragged their own prisoners to the top of the city's walls. They tore them apart limb by limb. Furious, Barbarossa ordered the hanging of forty hostages from Crema. Then he killed six noble knights who had been captured in a previous battle in Milan.

Of course, the people living inside castles under siege would fight for their lives. They would use long, forked poles to topple ladders—and the terrified knights trying to climb them. Defenders poured raw sewage, scalding water, boiling oil, or hot tar onto the soldiers below. Archers in castle towers rained down arrows on the enemy. Brave knights—on both sides— continued to fight to the bitter end.

3

The Road to Knighthood

Do you still want to be a knight? Not everyone could become a knight. First, you had to be a boy. Girls sometimes fought to defend their castles, but they could not become knights. Second, in many countries, future knights had to be born into wealthy (or noble) families. Poor peasants could become lowly foot soldiers, but not knights. The sons of nobles usually had two options: they could either train to become knights, or they could become monks or priests.

Paging All Knights!

Like today's Olympic gymnasts and figure skaters, knights started their training at a very young age. For a young boy, the road to knighthood was a back-breaking, tooth-cracking, bone-shattering ordeal. To become a knight, a noble's son had to learn to be tough. At the age of seven, he would be sent away to become a **page** in a nearby castle. A page was a servant to his new master, the lord of the castle.

Pages were expected to work hard. They ran errands and did chores. They waited on tables at mealtimes. Sometimes they carved the lord's meat. They carried basins of water for guests to wash their

19

hands. Like waiters, they served platters of food. They filled goblets with wine. Pages had to learn courtesy and patience. If they disobeyed, they often received beatings. Eventually, a page would learn how to defend himself.

Knights in Training

Handling weapons and horseback riding were often painful parts of training. Sometimes a page was flung from his horse. If he failed in sword fighting, an instructor might give him a painful whack with a sword. The key was to learn quickly!

Exercise and wrestling helped a page grow stronger.

Sometimes pages stomped around in heavy armor for hours to get used to the weight. When a page was ready, he would learn how to fight with a 10- to 14-foot lance. Mounted on a horse, the page charged at a **quintain**. This was a human-shaped dummy armed with a shield. It held a heavy weight. A quintain looked like a scarecrow dressed as a knight. Galloping at full speed, the page would try to strike the center of the quintain's shield with his lance. Then the quintain would spin. The page and his horse had to leap out of the way. Otherwise, they would be smacked by the dummy's weight. Ouch!

Another risky training activity was hunting. Killing deer, boar, birds, and rabbits forced young boys to learn survival skills. A wild boar could charge from behind bushes. It could slice open a hunter with its sharp tusks. A page would have to thrust his spear in a flash. While hunting, a page also learned how to find his way through dark, creepy forests. All of these skills would come in handy later on the battlefield.

Toil and Trouble

At age fourteen, a page became a squire. Training became much harder. A squire was a servant to a knight. He dressed the knight and polished his armor and weapons.

One way to remove rust was to load the armor into a barrel of sand and vinegar. The squire would roll the heavy barrel around until the armor was rubbed clean.

A squire took care of his knight's horses. He shoveled stinky manure from the stables. At bedtime, he would help his knight undress. Forget about resting. A squire often slept in the doorway of his knight's room. He was always ready to be called to service.

At first, squires practiced fighting by whacking a sword against a wooden post called a **pel**. Sometimes they carried swords that weighed about twenty pounds—twice the weight of swords carried in battle. This way, squires bulked up their muscles. Eventually they were ready to fight each other in practice drills. These exercises often ended with bruises and bloody injuries. Yet that meant a squire was ready for the gore of real war.

Squires went off to the battlefield with their knights. A squire would dress his knight in armor. He carried the knight's heavy weapons. In the heat of battle, some squires joined the fight.

Costly Equipment

If you survived the training, the road to knighthood had other challenges. Becoming a knight was very expensive. A strong warhorse could cost almost a year's salary. Because of the high

24

price of the metal, labor, and skill that went into making armor and weapons, suiting up a knight cost a small fortune.

Knights had to pay for their own gear. They either earned money from grants of land or they were paid to fight. Sometimes a knight's wealthy family had to pay the bill. Some knights also stripped armor and weapons from dead warriors on the battlefield.

Now and then, squires would seek out challenges to prove their bravery. Sometimes they achieved great honor. Other times, the results were tragic. In the late 1300s, French squire John Boucmel challenged an English knight to a joust. At the joust, the knight charged at Boucmel. His lance bounced off Boucmel's armor and pierced through his neck. The squire died instantly.

25

Graduation Day

Not every squire became a knight. Some simply couldn't afford the equipment. Others didn't have the right skills to become knights. Many knights-in-training spent their entire lives working as squires.

A squire who had proven his knightly skills could become a full-fledged knight by his late teens. Early on, new knights were simply presented with weapons and armor. Later, the declaration of knighthood became known as the

"**dubbing** ceremony." Sometimes this event was held with great fanfare.

Suits of Armor

In some ways, knights were the battle tanks of the Middle Ages. Riding on mighty warhorses, they would charge at the enemy. At the same time, they needed to protect themselves from heavy blows and the piercing stabs of sharp weapons. Metal suits of armor became the protective fashion of the time.

Mail Call

The first knights wore mesh body armor. It was made of hundreds or thousands of linked metal rings called **mail**. Knights wore mail face masks, neck guards, shirts, and even leggings. They sometimes added mail mittens to their sleeves. As you might imagine, wearing metal clothing could be downright painful. Metal heats up quickly.

It cuts into skin. So knights wore plenty of padding under the metal mail. A quilted garment called an **aketon** was stuffed with linen and horse hair for padding. For less well-off soldiers, the aketon was filled with itchy straw.

When heading into battle, knights wore a shirt of mail called a **hauberk** (HO-berk). Made of 30,000 metal rings, a hauberk could weigh 20 to 30 pounds. It was a heavy load to bear. Yet knights weren't taking chances. If they wore plain clothes or exposed bare skin, they could be hacked to pieces. The metal rings did a decent job of blocking the slicing blade of a sword. But a knight's bones could still be smashed if

When Mail Fails . . .

In 1361, the Danish army attacked an army of Swedish peasants on the island of Gotland. The Swedes were wearing mail armor. They were badly beaten by the Danish troops. After the battle, the bodies of about 2,000 Swedes were piled into mass graves. They were still wearing their armor. In the 1930s—about 570 years later—the graves were unearthed. It was discovered that spiked weapons had pierced the skulls of about 125 Swedes through their mail hoods. More than 450 peasant soldiers had been slashed with swords and axes. The wounded were "finished off" with blows from clubs and hammers. Their mail armor had failed them miserably.

he was struck with a heavy club. A strong blow could also drive the metal rings into the knight's flesh. If the rings caused an infection, the knight could die.

Perhaps the biggest drawback of mail was that it was holey! A sharp weapon could pierce through the mail's loops. Because of the poor medical care of the time, wounded knights could bleed to death. Obviously knights needed better protection. They started adding steel plates to their armor. By the fifteenth century knights had changed the style of battle gear. They wore head-to-toe suits of **plate armor**.

Men in Metal

Unlike mail, the smooth, solid surfaces of metal plate armor could deflect swords. The force of a heavy blow spread out through the armor. This would dull the impact. Since it was fashioned from iron and steel, plate armor might seem clunky and stiff. If you look closely, though, you can see how flexible plate armor can be. It was curved to fit over limbs. Hinges were placed at joints. The arms and legs were covered with small interlocking plates. They looked like scales of metal snakeskin. These features allowed knights to stomp around more easily.

Also, some armor had a small slot cut out of the front so the knight who wore it could go to the bathroom!

Metal helmets came in many shapes and sizes. Some helmets were curved with pointed ridges on top. These features helped deflect

30

the blows of a battle ax that could split open a knight's skull. Many helmets had visors to protect the face. A visor could be raised when a knight wasn't fighting. In 1370, an English knight named John Chandos made a fatal error. He forgot to lower his visor during a battle. A lance pierced through Chandos's skull and into his brain, killing him.

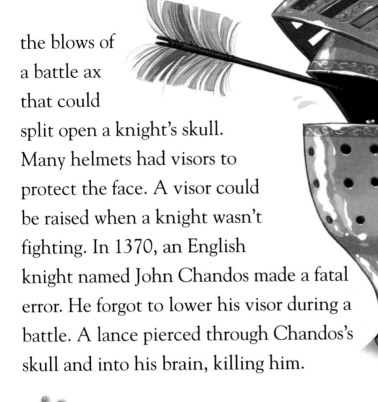

Did you know that the average American solider today carries about 60 to 75 pounds of combat gear? Not that much has changed!

Hot and Heavy

One drawback of plate armor was its weight. A full suit of armor weighed about 44 to 65 pounds. Carry around 10 six-pound bowling balls all day and you'll have an idea how heavy that can be. The difference between wearing heavy armor and lugging bowling balls, though, is that the weight of the armor was spread across a knight's body. A muscular knight was able to walk, mount his horse, and charge at the enemy while wearing a full suit of armor.

The weight of a knight's armor may have been tolerable, but the heat was deadly. You know how hot a car gets in August? Now imagine *wearing* the car in the blistering heat! Metal traps heat *and* smelly sweat. Add to this the quilted clothing knights wore under metal armor—and delete the

Hey, Rolf, Is That You Under There?

Suits of armor covered knights in metal from head to toe. So how could you tell one knight from the next? A colorful system of symbols and patterns was developed. The system became known as heraldry. These designs decorated shields, armor, surcoats (tunics), and banners. In the confusion of battle, heraldry helped knights find each other and join forces. Well-known symbols such as lions and dragons were meant to instill fear in the enemy. Heraldry was passed down in families.

deodorant (that wasn't invented until 1888)—and you're left with one hot, stinky soldier.

Knights sometimes covered their armor with a lightweight fabric tunic called a surcoat. It protected armor from rain and rust. It also reflected some of the sun's rays and provided some cooling airflow. However, many knights who escaped injury still fell victim to heat exhaustion. They became dehydrated and weak. In this sorry state, knights were often captured and held for ransom.

35

Weapons of War

During the Middle Ages, most battles were fought face to face. Early on, it was considered cowardly to sling rocks or shoot arrows from far away. Those were the weapons of peasants. Knights showed their strength and courage by fighting hand to hand. They depended on all sorts of weapons designed to pierce armor, crack bones, and clobber their enemies.

Other than his horse, a knight's best friend in battle was his sword. A sword enabled a knight to strike down his foe from the safety of his saddle. Swords were crafted from iron and steel. Some of them were double-edged. Knights swung these swords over their heads. They could tear metal mail links apart and rip through flesh. The sharp, pointy tips of **thrusting swords** were used to stab enemy knights between metal mail loops or joints in metal plates. Some swords were as much as 42 inches long.

To protect themselves, knights also carried shields. These were made of wood and covered with leather. Shields were ideal for times when knights got off their horses and fought on foot. The shields helped block arrows and clubs. Yet shields weren't always effective. A knight could drive a lance through his enemy's shield and armor. The lance would plunge deep

37

into the enemy's body. If the enemy was lucky, he would die quickly. Sometimes shields were held like stretchers. They were used to carry dead bodies off the battlefield.

Some knights attacked each other with axes. Using both hands to swing the ax, knights could hack off limbs or cut through torsos. They even cut through helmets and chopped off heads. Maces and **war hammers** were clublike weapons used to smash against armor. The spiky head of a mace was like a prickly steel pineapple. It could easily shatter bones. A knight sometimes stabbed his enemy with a sharp **dagger**. Daggers were mostly used when a knight had lost or broken his other weapons.

Knights had to be on the defensive. Archers tried to shoot them down using different kinds of bows and arrows. **Crossbows** were easy to aim. But they were heavy and they took a long time to reload. Some archers used **longbows** to shoot sharp arrows. Arrows could fly about 1,000 feet through the air. A skilled archer could launch up to 15 arrows per minute. Arrows would fall from the sky like stabbing shards of hail. A single arrow could cause a deadly injury. When French soldiers captured an English longbowman, they would chop off

his middle and index fingers. He would never shoot an arrow again.

Foot soldiers began using **pikes** against knights. These were 18-foot-long spears that soldiers used to stab horses and their riders. Rows of soldiers armed with pikes had a "porcupine effect" in scaring off knights. **Halberds** were also a knight's

The Battle of the Golden Spurs

In 1302, an army of citizens from a region called Flanders fought against French knights with a weapon called a "goedendag," meaning "good day." It was hardly a good day for the knights! A goedendag was a combination of a spear and a spiky mace head.

The townspeople used the goedendag's spear to pull the French knights from their horses. Then they would crush their armor with the mace head. In this battle, the Flemish took home about 700 pairs of spurs from dead knights as trophies. This clash became known as "The Battle of the Golden Spurs."

nightmare. These 8-foot-long weapons had blades that looked like meat cleavers. The back of the blade had a curved, clawlike hook. A soldier would use a halberd to hook a knight's armor and yank him off his horse. Once the knight was on the ground, the soldier would swing the halberd's blade. He would slash the knight through his helmet. Farewell, fair knight.

Goodnight, Knights

Knights lived though many hardships. They also caused unbelievable pain to others. Yet knighthood survived for about 1,000 years. In the sixteenth century, the era of knighthood began to fade. Part of the reason was that plate armor was becoming outdated. Pikes and halberds pierced through metal armor. What's more, a knight's armor could not hold up to the explosive force of the newest weapons: guns. Professionally

trained soldiers, rather than knights, took over the battlefields. Cannons blasted through castle walls.

Still, in the twenty-first century, the legacy of knighthood survives. Knights, or at least their images, seem to be everywhere. They show up as toys and in movies, books, and computer games. Even jousting has been kept alive at festivals, although it is a much safer sport today. Whether knights were violent, greedy, and cruel, or a model of honor and courage, one thing is clear: knighthood continues to spark the imagination.

Words to Know

aketon—A quilted garment worn under metal armor.

Black Death—An epidemic that killed 30 to 60 percent of the population of Europe during the Middle Ages.

crossbow—A weapon used to shoot wooden bolts.

dagger—A sharp, knifelike weapon.

dubbing—Ceremony in which squires were declared knights.

epidemic—A widespread disease.

halberd—An eight-foot-long weapon with a sharp blade.

hauberk—A metal mail shirt worn in battle.

heraldry—A system of colorful symbols and patterns used to identify knights.

joust—A contest in which two knights on horseback dueled each other with lances.

knight—A warrior who fights on horseback.

lance—A weapon with a 10- to 14-inch-long wooden shaft and a metal head.

longbow—A large bow used to shoot arrows.

mace—A clublike weapon.

mail—Mesh body armor made of linked metal rings.

melee—A mock battle in which teams of knights clashed against each other on horseback.

page—A young boy training to become a knight.

pel—A wooden post used to train squires in sword fighting.

plate armor—Armor made of iron and steel. Often, many pieces of plate armor were combined to make a suit of armor.

quintain—A dummy armed with a shield and a heavy club used to train pages and squires to fight with swords.

squire—A teenage boy training to become a knight.

surcoat—A fabric tunic worn over metal armor.

thrusting sword—A sword that could stab through metal mail loops or through joints in plate armor.

tilt—A wooden barrier that separated knights in a joust.

tournament—A mock battle in which knights competed to win riches.

war hammer—A clublike weapon.

Further Reading

Bouchard, Constance Brittain (chief consultant). *Knights: In History and Legend.* Buffalo, N.Y.: Firefly Books, 2010.

Gravett, Christopher. *Eyewitness Knight.* New York: Dorling Kindersley, 2007.

Hunt, Norman Bancroft. *Living in the Middle Ages.* New York: Chelsea House Publishers, 2009.

Internet Addresses

The Metropolitan Museum of Art
**http://www.metmuseum.org/
search-results?ft=armor+english**
(Read about and see different kinds of suits of armor.)

National Jousting Association
http://www.nationaljousting.com
(Find a jousting competition near you!)

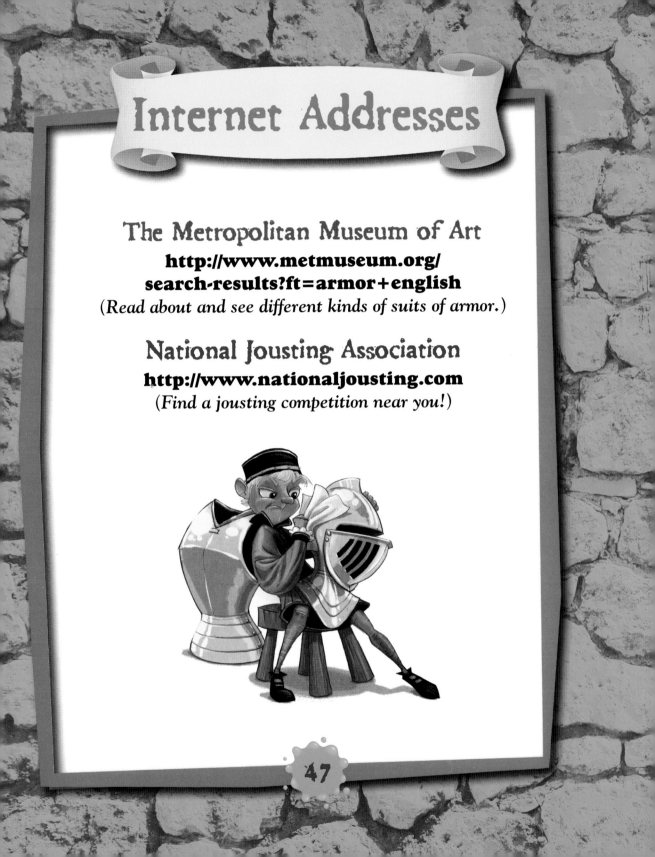

Index